SHARE YOUR Passion

7 Stages to Leverage Your Expertise & Make a Difference

By Renée Hasseldine

First published in 2015 by Eventology Pty Ltd
15 Green Place, Eltham, VIC 3095, Australia

© Renée Hasseldine and Eventology Pty Ltd
The moral rights of the author have been asserted.

National Library of Australia Cataloguing-in-Publication data:

Author: Hasseldine, Renée
Title: SHARE YOUR PASSION: 7 Stages to Leverage Your Expertise & Make a Difference/Renée Hasseldine
ISBN: 978-1-925884-23-4
Subjects: Business coaching, course creation, thought leadership

All rights reserved. Except as permitted under the Australian Copyright Act 1968 (for example, a fair dealing for the purposes of study, research, criticism or review), no part of this book may be reproduced, stored in a retrieval system, communicated or transmitted in any form or by any means without prior written permission. All enquiries should be made to the publisher at insert relevant email address.

Editor-in-chief: Georgina C.

Disclaimer:
The material in this publication is of the nature of general comment only, and does not represent professional advice. It is not intended to provide specific guidance for particular circumstances and it should not be relied on as the basis for any decision to take action or not take action on any matter which it covers. Readers should obtain professional advice where appropriate, before making any such decision. To the maximum extent permitted by law, the author and publisher disclaim all responsibility and liability to any person, arising directly or indirectly from any person taking or not taking action based on the information in this publication.

This book is for those people who dare to find their passion, live their passion & share their passion.

***

"Renée has always been one of the most passionate people I know. From her causes, to her clients, and more recently her family, Renée is passion personified. In this book she turns that passion to helping you get your message out into the world, and turning your good ideas into a course that can change lives and make you money."
Peter Cook, CEO, Thought Leaders

"Clearly Renée is an overachiever in the most wonderful way. She oozes passion. It's impossible not to get fired up and feel Renée's energy leaping off the pages. The real value comes from her super smart framework showing a step by step approach to developing a course on a topic that floats your boat."
Andrew Griffiths,
International Bestselling Entrepreneurial Author,
Speaker & Commentator

"One of those rare occasions that blends a very talented Girl with someone who is a great pleasure to work with."
Peter Sage, The Millionaires Business School

"My coaching career began as many do; trading time for money. Although I had great intellectual property I was struggling to turn that into a tangible product or curriculum. I felt stuck and came very close to quitting.

Then a friend introduced me to Renée. Working through the processes outlined in the book with Renée, I have been able to take my IP and create a curriculum that not only delivers excellent results for my clients but has allowed me to create a high 6 figure business. Renée has helped me create an eco-system of physical and digital products that serve my market. As we continue to add to the product mix, my expectation is that within 18 months our revenue will double.

This is a book whose time has come. Renée has put together a blueprint to build, quite literally, a million dollar business. Read this book but more importantly, take action on the material presented. It could just be the best investment you ever make."

Dr Jesse Green

"Renée is definitely one of the most efficient, effective and empowering people I have ever worked with in my business of 15 years. Renée appeared like an Angel to solve all my troubles! In six weeks she achieved what no other could in three years. When she needed me to make decisions to take the next step and I was lagging behind her schedule, she gently and powerfully gave me the encouragement I needed to get the job done. She's an absolute gem."

Monique Bevan,
General Manager, Sentient Being

TABLE OF CONTENTS

FOREWORD BY ANDREW GRIFFITHS .... **XI**

FOREWORD BY PETER COOK .... **XV**

INTRODUCTION **1**

IN THE BEGINNING **3**

    THE GREAT DEPRESSION 8
    FUCK WORK-LIFE BALANCE 12
    YOU HAVE A CHOICE 13
    YOU CAN DO IT TOO 14
    TURNING PASSION INTO PROFITS 16

LET'S GET A FEW THINGS STRAIGHT **21**

    PRINCIPLE 1: GIDDY-UP! 22
    PRINCIPLE 2: EVOLVE, EVOLVE, EVOLVE 23
    PRINCIPLE 3: GET IN THE ZONE! 25
    PRINCIPLE 4: INFOGRAPHICS RULE OK! 27
    PRINCIPLE 5: CHECKLISTS… YEAH BABY! 28
    PRINCIPLE 6: TRUST YOUR GUT! 28
    PRINCIPLE 7: JUST DO YOU! 30

THE 7 STAGES OF COURSE CREATION **33**

STAGE 1: PASSION & PURPOSE **35**

    WHY? 36

Who? 38
What? 39
Your Passion Sweet Spot 40

STAGE 2: BRAND 45

Passion & Purpose 48
Customer Experience 48
Brand Elements 49
Marketing 50

STAGE 3: PACKAGE & PLAN 51

Package it Up 52
Plan 61

STAGE 4: BLUEPRINT 63

Your Methodology, Your IP 64

STAGE 5: FRAME IT 79

Frame Your Modules 81
Get the Foundations Right 81
The Pillars 82

STAGE 6: BUILD IT 85

Structure 87
Template 91
Create 92
Combine 94

STAGE 7: DELIVER 97

Know your Audience 98
Build in Testing & Learning Over Time 99

    A Note about Learning Styles 101
    Keep them Awake 102

CONCLUSION 109

ACKNOWLEDGEMENTS 113

ABOUT THE AUTHOR 117

FIND ME ONLINE 119

ABOUT SHARE YOUR PASSION 121
    Our Purpose: 121
    Our Values: 121

RESOURCES 123
    7 Stages Checklist 123
    Marketing Checklist 123

WORK WITH ME 125

FOREWORD BY ANDREW GRIFFITHS

There's a lot of talk these days about finding your passion and following your passion, which is all kind of nice (well it is in fact wonderful) but surely the ultimate goal is to share your passion, turn it into a great business and make a sensational living out of it whilst helping others? Sounds perfect to me and that's what Renee Hasseldine has figured out.

If there is a book written or published on passion, I've read it. Most of them are great and in recent years they've transitioned into helping people to find their passion in a modern, crazy and complicated world. But I've always felt that something was lacking, specifically what to do with this passion once you've found it.

Sure, there were lots of big statements, visions, change the world quotes, but not a lot of real advice on building a great business by sharing what it is you're passionate about. Until now.

Clearly Renee is an overachiever in the most wonderful way. She oozes passion. Now her mission in life is to help people find their passion and share it with others. We all need a little help to figure out how to go about it and that's one of the things I love the most about this book.

"Share Your Passion" is certainly written as an inspirational book. It's impossible not to get fired up and feel Renee's energy leaping off the pages. The real value comes from her super smart framework showing a step by step approach to developing a course on a topic that floats your boat.

I love that Renee finds lists sexy, she has tamed the infographic as a source of powerful communication and she knows each and every one of the obstacles that stops people from sharing their passion.

I've had the great fortune of turning my passion into a way of make a living for well over thirty years. It has taken me around the world many times, put me in front of hundreds of thousands of people and given me the opportunity to work with some truly incredible people. If I had this book thirty years ago, I would have achieved all of this so much sooner.

My advice is simple. Read this book from cover to cover, non-stop. Then do it again. Follow Renee's advice, her framework and her wisdom. Notice how it feels, get a little uncomfortable, think bigger thoughts and calm the inner monkeys that are trying to talk you out of being all you can be and more.

Share your passion - because the world needs you to.

Andrew Griffiths
International Best-selling Entrepreneurial Author, Speaker and Commentator

FOREWORD BY PETER COOK

At Thought Leaders we've spent the best part of two decades helping experts get paid for their advice. Our mission is to help clever people be commercially smart. And to do this sustainably your practice needs to be about more than just money. It needs to be a labour of love - getting paid to do work you love with people you like the way you want.

As Renée says, we need to turn our passion into profits.

I've seen countless coaches and experts facing the problems that Renée identifies in this book.

Fundamentally sharing your passion as an expert – what we at Thought Leaders call running a thought leaders practice – is a very different game to running a business as an entrepreneur. If you are looking to build a business as an entrepreneur, you've probably picked up the wrong book. However if you are an expert looking to build a practice, keep reading.

The main challenge we face as experts running a practice is the well meaning, bad advice that we get from people who know the game of business, but don't know the game of building a practice as an expert. We need to make sure that we get our advice from people who understand the game we're playing.

And if you're an expert looking to share your passion, Renée is clearly one of these people. She gets the game we're playing.

In business you look for a hungry market, and then seek to fill that need. It's what you'll learn at business courses and at internet marketing summits. And it's not what we do.

As Renée says, as an expert, the thinking comes first. Start with what you know, with what she calls your *passion sweet spot*. Then think about whose problems that solves.

Renée has always been one of the most passionate people I know. From her causes, to her clients, and more recently her family, Renée is passion personified. In this book she turns that passion to helping you get your message out into the world, and turning your good ideas into a course that can change lives and make you money.

She has put together a step by step, paint by numbers process for taking that passion and getting it out into the world.

This is a book about making money *and* making a difference with your expertise and your passion. Enjoy.

Peter Cook
CEO, Thought Leaders

INTRODUCTION

Love what you do & do what you love.

Renée Hasseldine

INTRODUCTION

I have written this book to save you time. Seriously, none of this is rocket science and you're an intelligent human being. You could probably work all this stuff out for yourself. All you would need is time. Lots and lots of time. The information contained in these pages is based on years of experience working with clients, developing my own businesses... not to mention thousands of hours spent down rabbit holes, deepening my own knowledge, researching and integrating the best of what I learn from others, continuously evolving... and err, making mistakes.

I want to share it with you now so that you can save years of your own life, avoiding going round and round in circles trying to figure out what comes next! That way, you can get your unique message out there and leverage your expertise sooner rather than later. The sooner you launch your knowledge, the sooner you can make a difference. And I'm so committed to empowering you to make a real difference in this world.

IN THE BEGINNING

In the Beginning

I grew up in an entrepreneurial family. My dad has always run his own businesses, or run other people's businesses for them. Since my brothers and I were young, we've always been involved or exposed to what running a business takes. For me, business and work ethic were ingrained. Working hard and seeing what needs to be done is a natural instinct.

My earliest memories are of playing at Mitchelton Winery as a child. Dad was managing it and we were living on site. It was an awesome 'backyard' for a kid. We had emus, kangaroos and a swimming pool. There was a 55 metre tower with a lift in it. The cellars were a mysterious maze of tunnels to me as a child and I remember the smell of oak and wine as I explored them in wonder.

We had our own "house" on the premises, but sometimes we would eat in the main dining room. My memory is hazy, but there was definitely Pavlova! And there would be music and dancing. My dad has always loved to dance. And it was always a proud moment if I could outlast him on the dance floor.

There were a number of other businesses that we lived and breathed from the inside. The Continental Hotel on the corner of Russell and Lonsdale Streets in the Melbourne CBD, Alzburg Inn Resort in Mansfield at the base of Mount Buller and the Duke of

Windsor Hotel on Chapel St, Windsor. Through these businesses, I had work experience from the time I could walk. Small business was in my blood.

I'm not sure how I ended up studying Commerce/Arts at Melbourne Uni. Reflecting on it now, I guess I imagined myself in a highly paid corporate career, make a tonne of money and believing that would make me happy. If I'm honest, Dental Science was my first preference, and not because I love teeth. In fact, I am quite queasy at the sight of blood. But the teenage me assumed dentists made good money and so that was good enough for me.

During my university days I ended up working at a Public Relations company inside the Australian Ballet building, where the highlights were dressing up as Elmo for a Sesame Street Live photo shoot for a Melbourne newspaper and meeting Hugh Jackman who was starring in Sunset Boulevard at the time. Actually the free tickets to all the shows we represented was an awesome perk too!

Somewhere amongst the musicals and theatre, my Dad came to me and suggested I participate in the Miss Australia Awards. Seriously, I had no idea what was involved, but there was no way I was wearing bathers on stage. I was relieved to learn it was about raising money for people with disabilities through the Spastic Society of Victoria (now Scope) and that was something I could be part of. I acknowledge now that I was immature and narrow minded before this endeavour. It was an incredible growth experience to be part of an organisation whose premise was to empower people to reach their full potential and to "See the person, not the disability."

The Miss Australia Awards program also provided opportunities for my own personal and professional development and I ate that stuff up. After two years in the program myself, I ended up training and mentoring other participants. I think this was when I first started to realise how much I loved facilitating workshops and empowering people to shine. Looking back now, this is definitely a time in my life when my heart was singing. I was passionate and I had purpose. I knew I was making a difference and it felt good.

Not all my work experiences would bring me the same joy.

Still at university, where I was a terrible student, I was thriving in my work. I always felt I was learning far more in my work than I did sitting in lectures. In fact, I skipped many lectures and tutorials and slept through the vast majority of those I did turn up to.

I worked at IBM Global Services Australia and for the first time got to apply my small business experience and knowledge to the big corporate world. I analysed staff utilization and was responsible for the department's billing conflict resolution with Telstra. When I started there were about 90+ outstanding conflicts. I got this down to zero and kept it there every billing cycle.

I was engaged at a boutique CBD hotel as functions manager through a temp agency. When I turned up, they had weeks of unreturned messages lying on scrap pieces of paper all over my office. There were no systems in place and no running sheets for the functions that were booked. I was horrified. So I built them a database! I loved the opportunity to innovate—to create systems and leave a work place better than I found it. Perhaps it was with this role that my love of creating order from chaos with systems was borne.

To be honest, back then, I also liked the money. Plus dressing up in a suit and working in the CBD felt so grown up and important. It all seems so shallow and ego-based now, but that's just where I was at the time. I was young and had a lot to learn.

I worked at PricewaterhouseCoopers for three months over the summer before my last year of university. I excelled at my work and brought a lot of experience and work ethic to the table that other graduates didn't have. They offered me a graduate job but there was just no way I could go back. It was so tediously boring that I felt a part of me die when I was there. I was just one cog turning in a big machine, and I realised that I would rather be creating the machine. Creating the systems and processes that turned like the cogs in the machine. I am a creator and an innovator. Accounting and finance just did not do it for me.

The Great Depression

I finished university in November 1999 and was offered a graduate job with Andersen Consulting (now Accenture). As I wasn't due to start until April 2000, I took a summer job with an Internet start-up company. I was the only female and the only non-'tech' person in the company. I was soon promoted to Vice President of Commercial Operations and was being paid more than twice what Andersen's was offering me. Plus, my own office complete with mahogany desk and views of the MCG… this was all very good for my ego. We completed a back-door listing on the Australian Stock Exchange and my work was high-powered and fast-paced. I decided that I wasn't interested in becoming a battery hen in a cubicle at Andersen's and instead stayed where I was. I bought myself a car and along with a good friend I purchased a house in West Footscray.

At 23 I'd made it, right? I had a house, a car, a fancy job title, a fancy office, and lots of money. This was 'it'.

Ah no, this wasn't *it*. I was seriously depressed. My life had no meaning or purpose and I didn't see the point of being alive. I wanted to die and I actually thought about it a lot.

I recall walking into a friend's party during this time and despite being quite close with most of the people there, that day, I just wanted to crouch in the corner in the fetal position to rock and cry. When I felt that overwhelming urge, I knew I had to abort the mission. I got back in my car and drove straight home. I don't even know if anyone had seen me arrive or leave. Or if they had any idea what was going on for me. But I was seriously in a bad place and having few resources to deal with depression, I couldn't see an end to it.

I realised the corporate world was not for me. It didn't fit with me. I needed to find meaning and purpose in my life. I needed to believe that when I turned up to work or committed myself to a project that it was going to have a meaningful impact on the lives of many, and that I would continue to evolve for having been part of it. I had no idea what that meant or how to make it happen, but I knew I had get out.

So I did two things. I started my own consulting business and I decided to open a licensed café. The café was not a well-thought out decision. It was an escape plan. I was running away from something rather than towards something. It just seemed like an obvious way out because hospitality was in my blood. And maybe it would bring me closer to my family. Maybe then they would "get" me.

While I was in the frantic midst of preparing to open my new café, my housemate, Nigel dragged me along to a Tony Robbins event. Basically you can thank Nigel (or blame him) for the personal development junkie I turned into. Because really, this was one of those massive turning points in my life. I was severely depressed, and along with the awesome counselling and therapy Nigel would provide after work, he dragged me along to Unleash the Power Within. Yes, I was unleashed, but I had unfinished business with that café!

I soon realised that I was opening the café for all the wrong reasons, but I was too far down the track to stop the train. Plus, a bunch of family and friends had invested their hard earned money as shareholders in the business and I didn't want to let them down.

So there I was, the tee-totalling vegan, running a café and offering people water instead of their coffees and alcoholic drinks because I wanted the best for their health. I would coach people over the bar. I was trying to make the business fit in with my passion and values, but it wasn't good for business and it wasn't good for me – I was a square peg in a round hole.

There were some very cool aspects too. I loved providing a space for local musicians and artists to shine. Local artists held exhibitions and Taasha and Tristan would entertain us with their beautiful music on Saturday nights. Years later they won a couple of ARIAs with their band The Audreys. I felt honoured to be part of their journey to making it big!

But the café was never going to work. It never made any money but I learnt a shit load.

Firstly, if you're going to start a business, do it for the right reasons. Make sure it is aligned with your passion and purpose. Be certain that it is congruent with who you are and what you stand for. Please, save yourself the financial and personal stress and learn from my mistakes.

Second, know your market. Be absolutely clear about who your ideal client is and what they want. I wanted to be able to get good coffee in West Footscray where I was then living and assumed I wasn't the only one. It's true there were more people like me buying and moving into the area, but there weren't enough of us to make the business work. I built it and they did not come. I was about 15 years ahead of my time! You've got to be where your ideal client is. Perhaps things would have been different if

I had that café today. With the power of social media, I could build my own tribe online and pull them into my vegan heaven. But in 2001 none of that happened.

Thirdly, know yourself. Know the conditions in which you thrive. I love my freedom. I love being able to wander off and work anywhere, anytime. A shop front with set trading hours feels like prison to me and I vowed never to be chained to a shop front again. If you love to be outdoors, why get a job tied to a desk?

Fuck Work-Life Balance

The phrase work-life balance shits me. It implies that on one hand there is work and on the other there is life. That living and work are two separate things. That living happens outside of work. If you're not living when you're at work, what are you doing there? Dying? In jobs where I was not living my passion and purpose, I suppose it did feel that way. So fuck "work-life balance". It's all life. Life balance. Love what you do, do what you love. Living for Friday night drinks and the weekends is not enough. You deserve to live your passion and your purpose and you absolutely can.

Instead we should be striving for Life Balance. It's like spinning plates. If you've got 10 plates spinning on sticks, and you are focused on just one plate, what happens to all the others? They come crashing down right?

In the same way, if you spend too much time focusing on one area of your life, such as your career, all the others areas are neglected and can coming crashing down. Your health, your relationships, your emotional and mental wellbeing suffer.

The aim of the game is to get all the plates spinning at the same time. And this is not a "do-it-once" task.

You Have a Choice

I know what it's like to be in a corporate job that's not juicing you. Getting out of bed in the morning feels like hard work. And when you get to the office, you don't even want to be there. You know that there has to be more to life than this, but there's also the fear and uncertainty of what lies outside the concrete jungle.

You have a choice.

You can stay and be miserable. You wouldn't be the first and won't be the last. Sadly, many people stay in jobs they don't love. In doing so you will likely win the security of a pay check and a job title, but far more is lost by staying.

Or you can put on your big girl or big boy pants and follow your heart. It's your choice.

Whatever choice you make, you're the one that has to live with it. So choose wisely. When you're 80 years old looking back on your life, what do you want to see? What will you remember? What will be your legacy? How will others remember you?

You Can Do it Too

One day, Alitta was sitting on the train wearing her smart glasses and a suit on her way to work in Martin Place, Sydney thinking to herself "I'm pretending to be one of you but I'm not". Then she picked her moment and started blowing bubbles! Right there on a commuter train at peak hour, was a woman who looked like all the others, except for the plastic bubble ring and soapy water she was blowing around the carriage. People didn't know how to respond to her random act of joy, but they were unlikely to even crack a smile. It was 8am and they were already unhappy before their working days began. Realizing how unhappy she was in that world, she sold all her stuff, dropped the rest off at Vinnies and went to India! Now she's loving her life, speaking, coaching and teaching groups and individuals stress management and mindfulness, with a strong passion for mindful eating.

Rebecca (name changed to protect confidentiality) left her $170k/year sales and marketing career because she wanted to make people feel good and her job just didn't cut it. She had experienced sexual harassment as a child and then again at 19 and 25. She felt like if she stayed in the corporate world, all those experiences happened for nothing. She wanted to derive a more empowering meaning from what had happened. For her, that means helping others who've experienced trauma.

Nigel worked as a solicitor in general law, at IBM GSA, in conflict resolution, change management and database technology solutions. In the corporate world, he felt excited, but he also felt ugly. At times he felt pride and he also felt disappointed and inauthentic. He escaped the corporate world by going into the welfare sector. He worked with young offenders and with victims of child abuse and families who were separating. Now he's become a teacher, teaching what he's passionate about.

These people did it and you can do it too. I'm not suggesting it is an easy decision but it is a simple one. If you're not feeling fulfilled in your work, take a leap of faith and follow your heart. I dare you to follow your passion and purpose. Whatever that looks like for you. Life's too short to settle for a career that you hate.

And I know there's fear of the unknown. There's uncertainty. But feel the fear and do it anyway. I'm not saying be an idiot and jump before you assess your risks or do some research. Just be smart about what is real and what is imagined.

Turning Passion into Profits

Sure, it's one thing to take the plunge and ditch the grey suit for the great big world outside the concrete jungle. But then what?

You're a driven and motivated person. You've always succeeded at whatever you put your mind to. So even though there might be some fear and uncertainty creeping up, deep down, you know you've got this.

The reality is you've got bills to pay.

The ideal is to love what you do and do what you love. If you're going to share your passion and live your passion, how do you leverage your expertise to make a difference?

It's one thing to work one-on-one with clients providing your expert services, but when you can leverage that by working one-to-many, you can make a bigger difference and reach more people. You can make more money in less time, so that your life is balanced.

Since I became a mum, I've been even more selective with the "work" I do. And whilst it has been important for me to really love my work since my great depression, being a parent has taken that drive to the next level. If I'm going to be spending time away from my kids, it had better be for a damn good reason.

When I first became a mum, I thought I was going to be a full-time stay at home mum until they were at school. I love my kids and philosophically wanted to give them the best start in life. For a while, I thought that meant being in my full-time care. However, I soon realised that following my passion and purpose makes me a better human being. It makes me a better wife and a better mum. When I'm doing what I love, I'm happier and more vibrant, and I'm setting a great example for my kids to follow their hearts and dreams.

Here's the thing. You have a wealth of experience. You know a lot of stuff. In fact, you know so much, that you could probably talk for days and days straight without drawing a breath. With so many brilliant ideas whirling around in your mind, it can be difficult to work out which to focus on.

I've listened to people talk to me about the programs they are 'going to' create for over ten years. And they're still not done. It's not that they don't have anything to offer. Quite the opposite.

There's a lot to be done. And it's easy to get lost in your own thoughts. To go off on tangents and lose hours and days at a time down rabbit holes. You chop and change and go in different directions. Life gets in the way and weeks, months and even years pass you by.

When it seems like such a huge mountain to climb, we can resist taking the first step. And if there's a mountain range, how do we choose which one to climb first? And the biggest fear of all is that you'll get to the top of that mountain and realise it was all for nothing. That it was a huge waste of time. And when you're on top of that mountain staking your claim, planting your flag in the ground, the whole world can see you. There's nowhere to hide. Your deepest fear that it won't be good enough and you won't be loved can stop you making it all the way to the top or even from taking the first step.

But you're an achiever. You want to climb your mountain and take a stand. You want to choose your mountain, get to the top and realise it was all worth it. That by climbing to the top, you've paved the way for so many more to follow and that you're making a real difference your way. With authenticity and integrity. With passion and purpose. With real meaning.

So, if you're going to get to the top of your mountain, you have to decide which mountain you're going to climb and take the first step. Let this book be your Sherpa and guide you to the top. Stick to the process of the 7 Stages and you will get to the top of your mountain in the most efficient way ... and it will be a beautiful view from that vantage point. You will deliver your program and it will rock.

The Benefits of Developing Your Own Courses and Programs

I've been in the personal development industry since 2001. I've met a lot of superstar experts, coaches and facilitators, and I've also met a lot who are seriously struggling (with a smile on their face).

Here are the biggest obstacles of a typical struggling coach or expert:

"I coach everyone"
Seriously coaches without a niche and who say they can coach anybody usually end up coaching nobody. I've seen this time and time again. You *must* define your ideal client. Creating your own program using the 7 Stages outlined in this book will ensure you have a clearly defined target market.

Selling coaching not solutions
Most of your ideal clients aren't Googling or looking for "coaching". They have problems and they want solutions. If you want to help them, you need to provide them with what they're looking for. By work-

ing through the 7 Stages, you will get really clear about the solutions to your ideal clients' problems.

Lack of credibility and visibility

This has nothing to do with how fantastic your skills or expertise are. This is all about how you are perceived in the market place. Every man and his dog wants to call themselves a coach these days and quite frankly, if you want to shine, you need to "wow" your ideal clients with your unique brilliance. When you develop your own intellectual property and you have a system that you become renowned for, you gain serious credibility and visibility.

Limited income

Stuck trading time for money, most people calling themselves a coach don't make more than $10,000 a year from coaching. I know lots of people get into coaching because they want to contribute and make a difference, but the truth is, if they can't pay the bills, it isn't sustainable. Developing a course or program allows you to move from working one-to-one with coaches, to working one-to-many. Add this to the benefits listed above and you can see how creating your own courses and program seriously leverages your earning potential and gives you greater life balance.

LET'S GET A FEW THINGS STRAIGHT

Why, when we know that there's no such thing as perfect, do most of us spend an incredible amount of time and energy trying to be everything to everyone? Is it that we really admire perfection? No - the truth is that we are actually drawn to people who are real and down-to-earth. We love authenticity and we know that life is messy and imperfect.

Brene Brown

Let's Get a Few Things Straight

Below are my 7 Course Creation Success Principles:
1. Giddy-up!
2. Evolve, Evolve, Evolve
3. Get in the Zone
4. Infographics Rule OK!
5. Bring on the Checklists!
6. Trust Your Gut
7. Just Do You

Principle 1: Giddy-Up!

You don't have to be great to get started, but you do have to get started to be great.

Les Brown

Forget Perfection, Just Map the Journey and Get Started
Don't wait for the perfect time, the perfect place or the perfect you... Just start! Course Creation is a process. Your IP WILL EVOLVE! You will continue to make improvements, but you have to get started to create something fantastic. So just get started. Come on, I've already mapped the process for you, so you really have no excuses.

When you do get started though, don't make the mistake of jumping into Stage 6. Yes, I know you just want to build your course or product and you might think you can save time, but you really won't. I've seen it time and again. It is a sure fire recipe for thousands of hours down rabbit holes. This is a 7 Stage process for a reason and the order of it is no accident. Don't try to take short-cuts because you will regret it.

Like all solid buildings, you must have a solid foundation. If you want to create a product people will love, you must create a solid framework for your course by working through each stage of the process. And even if it looks like more work, I promise it will actually save you time.

Principle 2: Evolve, Evolve, Evolve

It is not the strongest of the species that survives, nor the most intelligent that survives. It is the one that is the most adaptable to change.

Author Unknown (although often incorrectly attributed to Charles Darwin)

This book is the result of my best thinking right now. But it is not perfect. I doubt it ever will be. Why? Because I believe in a growth mindset. I'm constantly learning and growing. However, if I wait until any of my work or products are perfect, I'll never complete or launch any of them.

So, I urge you to create your course with your best thinking today and launch it. Get it out there. You can always come back and revise it later.

Evolving your work involves testing and tweaking, and I recommend this at every stage of the process. It is about continuous improvement and growth.

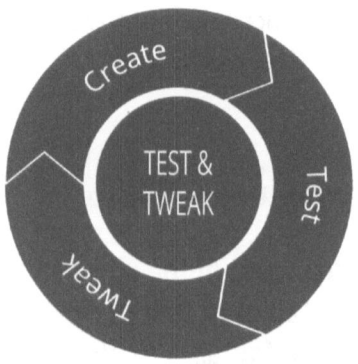

Here are some guidelines for testing and tweaking your content:
- ✓ Ask Your Tribe. Survey them and find out what they'd want covered, what's important to them, etc.
- ✓ Use the Process on Yourself
- ✓ Pilot the Process with Select Clients (and be honest that is what you are doing)
- ✓ Test it With Your Friends (as long as they fit your ICA)

- ✓ Use the Feedback you get from the Above to Tweak your product
- ✓ Create the next Version

Principle 3: Get in the Zone!

Let's have fun getting shit done.

Renée Hasseldine

Get In the Zone for Content Creation

Content Creation can go off on tangents and take as long as you let it. Get in the zone, follow the system and you will create something of true value in an efficient way.

Create the Space	Create the Mental and Physical Space you need to allow creativity to flow. This means removing all distractions, blocking out time in your diary, being in a place where you won't be interrupted and turning your phone off. Meditation, affirmations and writing a list of all other "to do" items for "filing" away can also assist. This should also mean having a buddy or a coach to hold you accountable.
Use your Body	Moving your body will help the energy to flow. Engaging your physiology in the creative process releases blockages. This can be as simple as standing up and using a whiteboard instead of sitting at your computer, or scheduling short intermittent breaks to stretch. You may be resistant to try this but I guarantee that if you stop for some whole body stretches, rebounding or a tapping every now and again you will remain fresher and more connected to your task overall.
Be Colourful	Use colour to highlight different ideas and thoughts, whether that is on a computer, a mindmap or a post-it note. It helps to create a more visual representation of your thoughts and colours also stimulate emotional energy – which is great for the creation process.
Soundscape It	Sounds that are conducive to the creative process include gentle natural sounds, like waves crashing or birds singing. Music can also stimulate and support your creativity. When selecting the soundtrack for your work, choose something that will get the juices flowing without distracting you. Don't look at me like that, TRY IT!

Flow	Don't censor yourself. Get it all out first. Do not edit as you go. No editing allowed until it is all written! As my dear friend and colleague Carolyn scribbled to me on a notepad at the back of a room during an event, we were born to F.L.O.W. (Freaking Love Our Work)!
Set a Time Limit	If you had to make a presentation at 9am tomorrow, you would be ready for it. Give yourself a time limit for completing your tasks and make it real by scheduling and publicising an event that you will need to be ready for.

Principle 4: Infographics Rule OK!

A picture tells a thousand words.

> Unknown

Now I'm revealing my inner nerd (maybe not so hidden and inner really), but years ago, I was truly excited by the power of a spreadsheet. I loved and thrived on creating spreadsheets that modeled complex businesses.

My latest nerd thrill comes from Infographics! Why use words when you can communicate your information in a picture? Ok, we still need to use words to explain or expand on the Infographic. But if you want to truly get your message across to people of various learning styles, then Infographics plus explanations is a seriously powerful combination.

Principle 5: Checklists...Yeah Baby!

I'm bringing sexy back.

Justin Timberlake

Okay, we've already established that I'm a bit of a weirdo, but I think checklists are sexy. There, I said it. I'm a checklists and bullet points kinda girl. I'm not into long-winded and flowery. I'm busy, you're busy. Let's just get straight to the point and get shit done okay! Let's make a list and make it happen.

Enough said.

Principle 6: Trust Your Gut!

You can't connect the dots looking forward; you can only connect them looking backwards. So you have to trust that the dots will somehow connect in your future. You have to trust in something - your gut, destiny, life, karma, whatever. This approach has never let me down, and it has made all the difference in my life.

Steve Jobs

Trust your gut instincts. If something doesn't feel right, listen to that feeling. Tune into it.

If I think back on mistakes I've made in business, most of them could have been avoided if I'd listened to my instincts.

How to Listen to Your Instincts
1. Close your eyes and centre yourself.
2. Take a few deep breaths.
3. Start scanning your body from head to toe and observe the sensations. When you feel an area that's asking for your attention, such as a tightness or tension or an ache or tingle, pause there and ask:
   - What does this part have to say?
   - What message does it have for me?
   - What lesson will set me free?
   - Is this the truth?
   - What else could be true?

Follow your instincts. That's where true wisdom manifests itself.

Oprah Winfrey

Principle 7: Just Do You!

Be yourself; everyone else is already taken.

Oscar Wilde

When I opened my café I was jumping in for all the wrong reasons. I learnt a valuable lesson about being true to myself and channelling my time and energy into pursuits that had real meaning for me.

Be authentic and congruent with who you are, your passion and your purpose. Be truthful. This has to start with you. And then, you must be true to your big why, speak to your tribe and make a real difference with the work you do.

I was having my legs waxed the other day and as Rebecca was finishing up she asked, "So what's on for the rest of the day?" "I'm heading back to work," I replied with a smile. It was a beautiful day outside and she seemed genuinely disappointed for me. "Oh that's a shame," she said. "No way! I love my work!" I said enthusiastically. Rebecca looked confused.

Seriously, choose a path that makes your heart sing. Choose to do something that you will enjoy, even when it's a beautiful sunny day outside!

There's no way I would have been able to respond like this back in my previous life in the corporate world. I lived for the Friday nights when I could let it all go and numb what was really going on with a few drinks and wild dancing on bars. I wished away my week days longing for the weekends. And even then, the weekends stopped feeling great, because I wasn't feeling great. I lived in dread of Monday.

Don't be beige. Do what you love. Your way. People can copy what you do but they can't copy who you are.

THE 7 STAGES OF COURSE CREATION

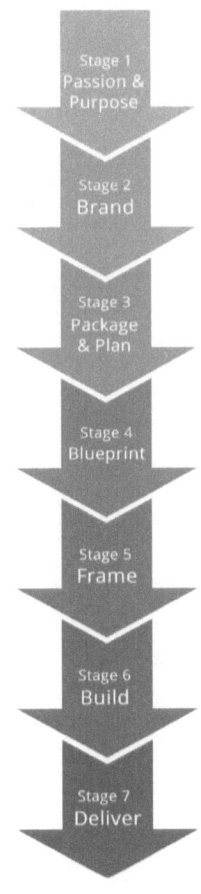

STAGE 1: PASSION & PURPOSE

Discover your Passion Sweet Spot and then live it, breathe it and share it.

Renée Hasseldine

Stage 1: Passion & Purpose

Stage 1 is crucial to getting the foundational stuff right up front. Otherwise you might end up with a program you don't love or a product nobody wants. Even if you just want to jump in and start creating the content, I guarantee that the time and effort you invest in this stage now will reap the rewards many times over through the growth of your business.

Why?

Don't ask what the world needs. Ask what makes you come alive, and go do it. Because what the world needs is people who have come alive.

Howard Thurman

STAGE 1: PASSION & PURPOSE

In his 2008 TED Talk, Gary Vaynerchuk says "There are way too many people in this room right now who are doing stuff they hate. *Please stop doing that!* There is no reason in 2008 to do shit you hate!"

Aaah Gary - I couldn't have said it better myself!

Make a stand for something and do it loud and proud. Love what you do and do what you love. Life is good when you can put your hand on your heart and know you're making a difference. That you're leaving a positive footprint in the world, not only through your work, but in your everyday life lived authentically and passionately.

So what is your purpose? What are you passionate about? What could you spend all day long doing with a smile on your face? What ideas, activities, challenges do you get out of bed for, and would happily keep you up all night?

If you didn't need money, what would you spend your days doing? I mean after the first stage where you lie around on the beach sipping cocktails. What do you decide to do with your time when that gets boring and your drive to add value and make a difference kicks in?

When this lifetime is over, how do you want to be remembered? What will be your legacy?

Action:
- ✓ Define Your Purpose
- ✓ Define Your Values
- ✓ Define Your Vision
- ✓ Set Your Goals
- ✓ Write Your Compelling Story
- ✓ Make Sure You're in Your Passion Sweet Spot

Who?

Don't try and be all things to all people. You'll end up being nothing to nobody.

Renée Hasseldine

Many people have resistance to defining who they want to work with. They feel constrained and restricted by narrowing down their audience down to their Ideal Client Avatar. It brings up fear and scarcity.

Choosing an Ideal Client Avatar is not taboo like choosing a favourite child. It's going to be okay. Really. It is.

Defining your Ideal Client will not limit you. On the contrary, it empowers you to own your zone. The more specific and clear you are about who you want to work with, the more they will feel like you are the right fit. That you are the one that can help solve their problems and provide the solutions they need. Because when you know who your client is, their problems and fears, wants and aspirations, you can speak directly to them. They feel understood and connected and that you know who they are and exactly how to help them.

When you know your audience intimately, you can deliver the content. Because you know your stuff. You're an expert. Nailing your ideal client gets you clearer on which parts of your expertise and brilliance are going to be the most relevant and add the most value.

Action
- ✓ Define Your Ideal Client Avatar. Be Specific.
- ✓ Identify Their Problems
- ✓ Identify Their Greatest Fear
- ✓ Identify What They Want
- ✓ Identify Their Greatest Aspiration

What?

Your purpose in life is to find your purpose and give your whole heart and soul to it.

> Gautama Buddha

Having clarified your 'Why' and your 'Who', determining the problems you solve and the solutions you provide becomes pretty obvious. It is so important to be clear about this because your clients aren't Googling you or your business name. When they're Googling, they're researching their problems and they're looking for what they think will be their solutions. So you have to be able to talk to them in a language they understand so that they can find you.

Action
- ✓ What Problems Do You Solve?
- ✓ What Solutions Do You Provide?

Your Passion Sweet Spot

So you've defined your Why? Who? And What? The final part of this stage is to make sure it's in your Passion Sweet Spot. How do you decide if it is the right thing for you? There are 5 key elements that need to align to reach and sustain your Passion Sweet Spot. I can't stress this enough…don't go taking short cuts here or skipping one of the elements, or you'll find yourself in pain sooner or later. Take it from me. I've been there, done that.

STAGE 1: PASSION & PURPOSE

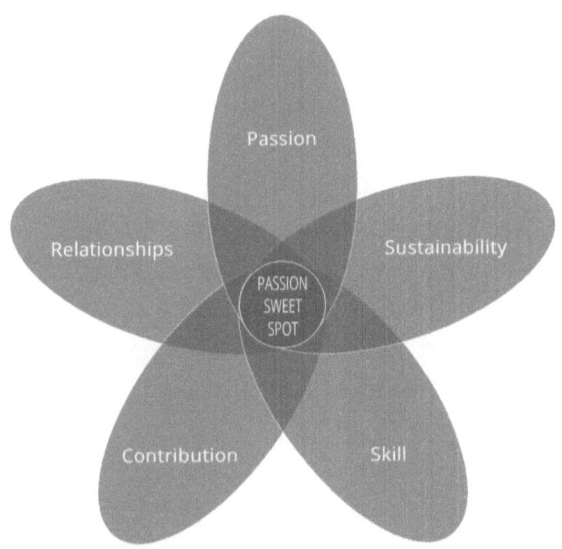

1. Passion
Check in. Are you really passionate about it? If you're not sure, find out more information. Speak to others who are already doing it. Then listen to your gut instinct. If you need to, refer back to the technique I described earlier to tune in.

2. Sustainability
Is it sustainable? Is it good for you? Does it serve you on a physical, mental, spiritual, emotional and financial level? This should happen both directly through your role and indirectly by providing life balance.

3. Skill
Do you have the expertise and skills to pull this off?

It's okay if you have some gaps in the content you want to cover. You can bridge these gaps yourself. Or you can draw on the skills of others.

Sometimes it is appropriate to undertake further study. As long as you are not just using the study as a further excuse. If you have a tendency to feel like you'll be ready when this and you'll be ready when that, and that tends to be a pattern for you, then check in and trust your gut instinct.

You don't have to be the one with all the skills and all the answers. You can interview experts. Be the conductor of the orchestra. There is beauty and skill in conducting. Get the ego out of it. You don't need the credit.

Just get real, then get moving.

4. Contribution
Are you making a valuable contribution to an organisation, a cause or people that you care about? You don't have to be trail-blazing a global cause, or setting out to change the world, but you do need to know that you are genuinely adding value and making even a small difference in the area you are passionate about. The sense of satisfaction will bring you joy and keep you motivated to continue.

5. Relationships

Is it great for your relationships? Does this passion and purpose allow you to be the best that you can be so that your personal and professional relationships thrive? Are you likely to be working with people with whom you share mutual respect and a sense of community?

In order to arrive in your Passion Sweet Spot, each of the key elements must be in balance. Remember balance looks a little different for each of us, and in order to find it we must each be willing to explore, juggle a little and arrive at the right spot in which these 5 elements bring us personal harmony. The minute we tip the scale, or forget that balance is dynamic and ever changing, harmony is lost.

This plan doesn't guarantee you 'happily ever after' but following it will ensure you are stepping up to create a life you love every day. Your life is not meant to be about working hard for someone else's fun and profit. Work is but one aspect of this crazy, amazing journey, and by honouring yourself with work that you are truly passionate about, you are giving yourself the greatest chance of a prosperous and joyful endeavour.

Action

Reflecting on your Why? Who? What?
- ✓ Are you Passionate about it?
- ✓ Is it sustainable?

- ✓ Do you have the skills?
- ✓ Are you making a contribution?
- ✓ Is it good for your relationships?

Want the full 7 Stages of Course Creation action checklist all in one document? You can download it at shareyourpassion.com.au/7-stages-checklist

STAGE 2: BRAND

Your branding is like the wrapping you put around your Passion & Purpose.

Renée Hasseldine

Stage 2: BRAND

Your branding is like the wrapping you put around your Passion & Purpose. It is how you "dress it up" to look pretty and appeal to your tribe.

But it is pointless wrapping an empty gift.

The wrapping has to reflect the gifts inside.

Have you ever been into a restaurant that looks wonderfully inviting and the staff are knowledgeable and friendly, but then the food, well, let's just be polite and say it's not so great. The wrapping is great, but what's inside quick frankly sucks.

On the other hand, we've all experienced those secret little gems. The dingy looking place that nobody dares enter, but when you eat the food it blows your mind. It might be your awesome little secret, but for the business owner, they're not doing themselves any favours. Not everyone is as brave as you for giving them a go. The wrapping turns many people off and the business will never reach its full potential.

You've got to be really clear about who you are and what you stand for before you go wrapping it up and designing a logo. Look, I'm a passionate, excitable woman. I know the temptation to get a gorgeous logo designed when you decide to start a new business.

But you'll be paying the price later if you jump in and do this too soon. Make sure you've absolutely completed Stage 1 – Passion & Purpose before you embark on Stage 2 - Brand.

I'm watching you.

Well I'm not really, but your clients are and we don't want them to be confused or turned off by an ill-fitting brand statement. Suffice to say, you should picture me shaking my finger at you if you are even slightly tempted to jump in and get a logo designed before you've gotten clear on your gifts.

It is so much more than a logo.

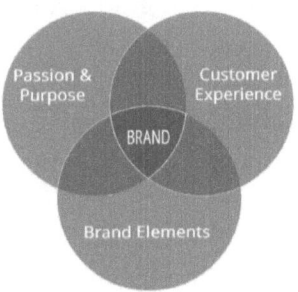

As you can see from the diagram above, I like to see a brand as the meeting of your Passion & Purpose, your Customer's Experience with you and your business and your Brand Elements, which includes things like your logo, fonts, colours, personality traits, brand essence, key messages and tagline.

Branding shouldn't be a long winded expensive affair, and less is usually more. But it should be an elegant representation of you and what you bring to the world.

Passion & Purpose

You need to position yourself so that clients look at you and relate. However, it is important that your branding is authentic to you and your 'Why? Who? What?'

We've already covered your Passion & Purpose AND I want you to keep this in mind for the rest of the process. It's not a do-it-once and shelve it exercise. Keep referring back to it. Let it guide you through all that you do.

Remember: People can copy what you do but they can't copy who you are. Just be yourself.

Action
- ✓ Make Sure Your Brand Aligns with Your Passion & Purpose (Why? Who? What?)

Customer Experience

Your customer's experience with you is a collection of interactions—moments of connection. Every social media post, email, phone call, group call and face-to-face interaction.

It is in these moments of connection that you can make a difference. Map out the moments of connection or touch points your clients have with you and your business, and determine how you want them to feel in each of these interactions. Then plan how you aim to make it happen.

Once you have completed your 'map', look back on the whole experience. Is anything missing? What else can you do to make their experience remarkable? How will you show them the love? This is your tribe. Your people. From your heart, demonstrate that you truly care about them.

Action
- ✓ Map Out Your Customer Experience

Brand Elements

These are the brand elements you've gotta get clear on. Not much more to say really. Just get it done.

Action
- ✓ Define Your Brand Elements:
  - Personality Traits
  - Brand Essence
  - Colours
  - Fonts

- Key Messages
  - Tagline
  - Logo
- ✓ Create a Brand Guidelines document detailing your Brand Elements

Want the full 7 Stages of Course Creation action checklist all in one document? You can download it at shareyourpassion.com.au/7-stages-checklist

Marketing

The marketing of your course is outside the scope of this book, but I cannot emphasise how critical it is to get this right. To that end, I encourage you to start with the awesome checklist that I have created for you online. You know how much I love a checklist!

You can get the Share Your Passion Marketing Checklist now at www.shareyourpassion.com.au/marketing-checklist

STAGE 3: PACKAGE & PLAN

Build your packages around what your tribe needs and the solutions you provide.

Renée Hasseldine

STAGE 3: PACKAGE & PLAN

Package it Up

Let's reflect on what you've done so far (since I know that none of you are taking short cuts or doing the steps out of order):
- You've got your big why sorted.
- You know who your tribe is.
- You understand and have articulated what their problems are and how can you solve them.
- Your branding is all mapped out.

What fantastic progress you're making. Stick with it.

Now it's time to think about how you're going to package your brilliance and deliver to all those eagerly awaiting it.

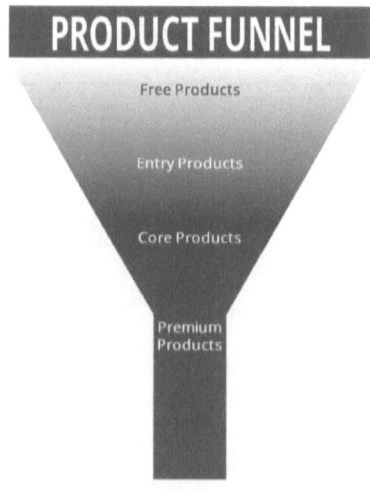

STAGE 3: PACKAGE & PLAN

A product funnel is an excellent tool for developing a systematic relationship between your products, and for clarifying (to you and your customers) how your products fit together. It also gives you the confidence to know what the next step is for your client.

There are many ways to be right here, but perhaps the easiest way for me to explain it is to demonstrate how it works for me. The main stream of my product funnel is based on my 7 Stages, which you can see in bold in my own funnel diagram and I've also listed below. When you're transitioning from offering your 1:1 services to leveraging your time and expertise to provide one-to-many services, this suite of products offers a simple and clear entry point from which you can build on later.

- Free Product: Checklist
- Entry Product: Discovery Session $99
- Core Product: VIP Group Program $660
- Premium Product: Retreat $4999

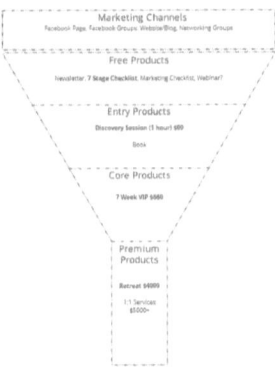

Marketing Channels

Okay so at the top we've got the widest point of the funnel, the largest catchment area of potential clients, 'marketing channels'. These channels include (but are not limited to):

- my Share your Passion Facebook page
- my Facebook group "From Corporate World to Conscious Entrepreneur"
- other Facebook groups where my Ideal Client hangs out
- my website / blog
- real life networking groups

I don't need to discuss these too much here, but I will say this. If you're anything like me, you don't want to be the sleazy sales guy.

So don't be.

In the online world, that looks like someone who pops into a Facebook group with their sales message and then disappears.

Choose a few Facebook groups and spend quality time in there adding real value and building real relationships. Hot tip: The way to not be seen as the sleazy sales guy... drumroll please... is to NOT be the sleazy sales guy.

Just be you. And show how you can add value and make a difference by answering people's questions.

Share your journey and "humanness". Do this authentically, in a way that is congruent with your Passion & Purpose and it will naturally resonate with the people who you want to work with.

Once people connect with me through these channels, if they are interested, they'll probably check out my website where there will be a clear call to action.

Free Products
Years ago someone told me that the purpose of your website is to collect names and email addresses. This simple advice has stuck with me and I come back to it often.

Think of it this way – when you're searching for something online, how many sites do you look at? And when you've made it to the end of your search, do you remember the first site you looked at? The second? The third?

It's unlikely that when you're searching for a solution to your problems, that you remember all the sites you look at, right?

But imagine if one of those sites had an irresistible checklist that addressed your immediate problem. A checklist that you were happy to provide your name and email address for. You receive the checklist and you think "wow, wow and wow. This person knows their shit."

Then, they continue to build the relationship with you, providing even more value via email. You feel heard and understood, not abused and harassed. So, when you're ready to take the next step, this person is most likely the expert you turn to, because you already know, like and trust them.

So, in my case, this is my Seven Stage Checklist. It is an opt-in on my website that adds massive value. I've laid out my whole process for course creation in one document. I haven't held back. Truly, it's all in there. And I'm not afraid to give it all away because I'm so confident that I have so much more to offer my clients. And you should see it this way too. Don't be afraid to give away too much. The more I give, the more people want to work with me.

Once people opt-in to my checklist, they are on my database and I can continue to show them the love and add massive value via email. You'll see I've got webinar in there with a question mark, because I'm not running them at the moment and I'm not that excited about running them for now. I know lots of people who are using these really well, so it is something for you to consider.

Webinars can be highly effective tools because they provide a forum in which you are able to connect with a group of prospects. It's an opportunity for people to hear your words and taste your passion and even ask their questions in real time, thus building trust further. If you've done well, the right prospects will be ready to take action at the completion of the webinar.

Entry Products

For people who love your free offering(s) and want more, you need an entry product. This is a low-cost entry point. This is where you can test who is actually willing to pay for what you have to offer. When it comes to entry products, I generally aim for less than $100.

A one-hour discovery session offered via Skype is a great way to add value and demonstrate your expertise. Being a live one-to-one call, it also builds the relationship. If your core product and premium product are high end, then having a real personal connection and conversation at this point will really aid the decision making process.

Importantly a one-on-one interaction also gives you an opportunity to confirm that this prospect is a good fit for you and what you have to offer. Past experience has shown me that many newcomers overlook this critical step in their haste to sign up clients and gets bums on seats so to speak. If your program includes ongoing personal contact (via phone, Skype, in person or at live events) then I urge you to screen your clients. The last thing you need is a client who is not a great fit emotionally in terms of their expectations as this inevitably leads to headaches for you, demands for refunds and even tarnishing of your otherwise wonderful reputation in an out-of-control social media space. Do yourself a favour and be fussy!

From the client's perspective, this is a low-cost and therefore low-risk way for them to test you out and see what you're made of. So, it really is a win-win solution.

You can always add more entry products, but for low-hanging fruit and quick wins, I would recommend a Discovery Session.

Core Products
Running a VIP group program is a great way for clients to move forward from the Discovery Session. It can be a great way for them to get access to you and what you have to offer, for a fraction of what it would cost them to engage your 1:1 services.

From your perspective, running a live group program gives you a great opportunity to test and tweak your content. You can even run a "pilot" for a lower cost than you plan to offer it later. If you structure each call to have content delivery plus live Q&A, the participants get great value and you get to learn, by their questions, what they really want and need and how you might be able to further improve your content. However, another word of caution here – if you're running a pilot program, don't go bending yourself out of shape trying to satisfy every little issue with each of your clients, and thinking you have to re-create the whole program to suit them. Your job here is to find the right balance between serving your clients with awesome value and support, and staying aligned with your own well thought out mission.

Overall, when done well, a pilot program provides you with an immediate feedback loop, and the opportunity to iron out problems and evolve your offering quickly. You may also find that you are well-placed to develop a more hands-off online course if you so wish.

Premium Products
The premium products in my own funnel are either my 5 Day Retreat, a personalised live event where we work through each of the 7 Stages, or my 1:1 Services. Insofar as the latter services are concerned I prefer to work with one or two clients at a time in this way and I'm generally at capacity through word of mouth. That's one of my main reasons for developing the one-to-many offerings and it's probably one of your drivers too.

So, if you want to keep (or start) offering your 1:1 services, then this is where you'd place it in the funnel. If you also want to offer a live workshop or retreat, that could go in here too.

Action

- ✓ Outline Your Product Funnel with offerings at different price points:
  - Free
  - Entry Products
  - Core Products
  - Premium Products
- ✓ For each Product outline:
  - Delivery Method
  - Timing & Duration
  - Support (if applicable)
  - Price

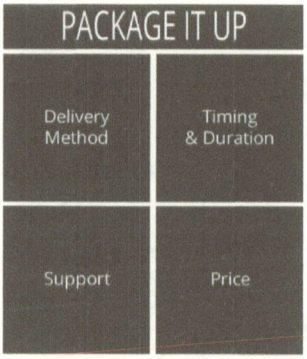

Here are some guidelines for packaging your offerings:

- ✓ Base your packages on what your ICA wants and the solutions you provide
- ✓ Focus on the benefits to your ICA rather than the features when offering it
- ✓ Create subscription-based programs for continuous cash flow

- ✓ Leverage your time by including information packages and group sessions (e.g.: webinars, group coaching, online courses, email courses)
- ✓ Put your personal one-on-one attention only into the highest level offerings
- ✓ Set fees based on outcomes rather than the effort you put in (so no hourly rates)
- ✓ Offer a money back guarantee

Plan

If you fail to plan, you are planning to fail!

Benjamin Franklin

I don't mean to preach to the converted here. I know that you know the importance of planning. So I don't need to go on about it. It is poignant to say don't be like the plumber with the leaky tap. You have to work on your business, and not just in your business. You have to assign tasks for your own progress and evolution, follow up, and stay on track. Schedule it. You know what to do. So do what you know and put in the time and effort to plan effectively.

Action

- ✓ Create Your Marketing Materials in Alignment with Your Brand

- ✓ Develop a Plan to Build Your Tribe (Refer to the Marketing Checklist)

Annual Planning
- ✓ Set Dates for your Workshops, Webinars, Group Coaching Calls, Holidays, Launches, etc. Remember to block out public holidays and other important events.
- ✓ Set Targets for:
    - Annual Income
    - Number of clients for each product
- ✓ Schedule Your Big Action Items (use this checklist and the marketing checklist)
- ✓ Do a Content Marketing Brainstorm
- ✓ Create a Content Marketing Schedule for the Year
- ✓ Create a Budget

Monthly Planning
- ✓ Plan & Schedule Your Content Marketing & Product Launches in your Monthly Planner

Weekly Planning
- ✓ Plan & Schedule Your Marketing Activities using a Weekly Content Marketing Schedule

Daily Planning
- ✓ Use a Daily Planner to focus on What's Most Important

Want the full 7 Stages of Course Creation action checklist all in one document? You can download it at shareyourpassion.com.au/7-stages-checklist

STAGE 4: BLUEPRINT

Create and develop something that you stand for and are known for.

Renée Hasseldine

Stage 4: Blueprint

Your Methodology, Your IP

Yay – Stage 4. This is the stuff that I get juiced about. This is the part where you create and develop the framework and methodology that you stand for and will become known for. Everything has become so clear for me and my clients since I defined my 7 Stages.

I've been creating and developing systems and programs like this since 2003 when I worked with Jan Spaticchia to build the highly successful *énergie* group from his living room. We sat on grassy knolls in the sunshine for our blue-sky thinking. It was an exciting and innovative time. From those humble beginnings, the *énergie* group is now an award winning market leader in the UK and it could be argued that its results guaranteed *émpower* program is the foundation for their success.

If you've ever joined a gym, you've probably experienced the standard scenario. You're given a tour, some measurements are taken and a trainer writes you a program, which they run through with you once.

Now if you're not a seasoned gym junkie, the next time you head back into the gym things might not go to plan. You walk in feeling a bit awkward. You don't know anyone and everyone else seems to know what they're doing. You pull out your program and see "lat pull downs". You think to yourself "Nope. Don't remember what that means." You feel way out of your comfort zone, and so you turn around and head back home, never to return.

Or maybe you're one of the brave ones that make it past the uncertainty of those first couple of workouts. Maybe you know what you're doing, so it's not quite so scary and you get past the first few weeks.

And then it happens. Your alarm goes off at 6am intending for you to head into the gym.

You press snooze.

Fuck it. You're not going. You'll go tomorrow.

The next morning your alarm goes off again at 6am and guess what? You press snooze again.

And that's the end of that gym membership.

You see, your gym might have the best equipment and best trainers in the world. But if you haven't dealt with the underlying causes of why you push that snooze button, then chances are you're not going to continue with that fitness club membership.

It's not a great scenario for you or your fitness. It's also a huge problem for a fitness club's business model.

Member retention is a massive ongoing issue for most clubs and the **émpower** program I created for énergie fitness clubs was revolutionary. Not only did it offer five weekly half hour sessions to build confidence, support progress and establish the exercise habit, it was also the first time that a fitness club addressed the underlying beliefs that can lead to pressing snooze instead of getting up and working out.

The program was **systemised** and then **humanised**. And that's the aim in building your system, your intellectual property. Having your own methodology that you are famous for is seriously powerful.

When I say to you: *The 7 Habits of Highly Effective People*, straight away, you know I'm referring to the work of Stephen Covey. 'Apple' and Steve Jobs are synonymous for stylish, must-have technology. Do you think people lined up outside a store for the latest computer before Apple pushed their sexy arses onto the IT scene? In my day, we may have spent the night lining up for tickets to see Madonna, but certainly not for a new personal device!

It all starts with one individual believing in themselves and getting absolute clarity as to how they are going to take that to their client demographic. Without a doubt, you have within you, the brilliance, the knowledge, and the expertise to create your own unique intellectual property that develops its own following.

This is your opportunity to create a legacy. A body of work that outlives you and continues to serve beyond your years on this earth. Now I don't want to scare you with making this into some huge thing that will overwhelm you. You don't have to re-design the Internet. Indeed, it is the simplest of methodologies which will connect with people and last. It is the sharp ideas, beautifully positioned to the right audience that will get the message across and make a real difference.

So, dare to put the complex web of your thoughts and brilliance into a clear and concise framework and you will reach more people. Your contribution will be magnified and your expertise leveraged.

In the process of developing your intellectual property, there are a number of Blueprint elements that will give you a good head start. And each of them will need an infographic!

You will develop more models and infographics as you create the modules in the program, however these first few elements will set you on the clear path to creating your own intellectual property and unique systems.

All the key elements of your blueprint should comfortably sit within and be aligned with your brand.

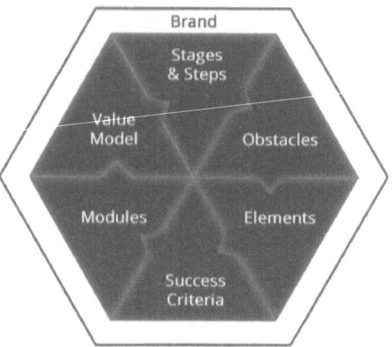

Value Model

Your Value Model illustrates possible scenarios for your clients, showing where they are likely to start off and where they would like to end up. It allows people to see where they are up to in their journey and where they aspire to move to.

The example below shows the wholehearted living value model, with the unconscious stream on the left and the conscious stream on the right.

STAGE 4: BLUEPRINT

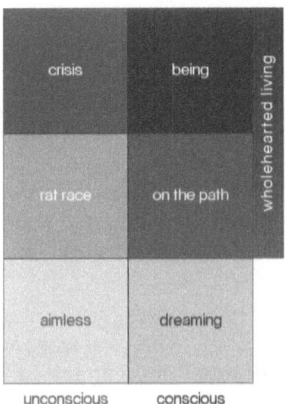

Aimless — In this phase you don't know what you want to do with your life so you just plod along with the day-to-day. In this phase life can be quite be quite fun for a while. There is no search for meaning or a desire to go deeper. You may want to keep your options open believing that this equates to true freedom. An example of someone in this phase is a teenager partying. They might be having fun (probably superficially) but they're going nowhere and the lifestyle is not sustainable. You may also end up back here in retirement if you haven't developed a sense of true self and created your purpose.

Rat Race — This is the phase of should, musts and living by what other people - such as parents, teachers or peers - say or think. In this phase there's lots of action being taken doing lots of stuff hoping it will make you happy in a job or business you don't love because you're paying off the mortgage and/or supporting your family. You may even be considered a great "success" by the people around you but you feel an "emptiness" or like something is missing in your life.

Crisis	When you're living an unconscious life when life's challenges arise as they always do it feels like a crisis. For example, a mid-life crisis, quarter life crisis, depression, loss of a loved one or other significant emotional event or trauma. Of course the crisis will pass but you'll end up back in the rat race if you're moving away from a situation rather than towards your true purpose.
Dreaming	The first phase in the conscious stream is Dreaming. You know what you want and probably spend plenty of time thinking and talking about it... but you're not actually doing anything about it. Fear is probably your greatest challenge - worried what others will think, the risks, money, fear of failure, fear of success, etc. Or perhaps you are waiting for the universe to deliver the dream on a golden platter.
On the Path	You know what's in your heart and you're living it, taking deliberate and wise action, living at cause. You're growing, learning and making a difference. True happiness prevails.
Being	When you are in the Being phase, you have a deep sense of purpose, meaning and self and feel true happiness and fulfilment. Life flows when you are in this phase because you are living as your true self, congruent with your purpose, values and highest vision of yourself. You're growing, learning and making a difference. You are an inspiration to others just for being you.

How will you represent your value model to your Ideal Client Avatar?

STAGE 4: BLUEPRINT

Stages & Steps

Stages & Steps illustrate the process or journey for your clients. For example, the Share Your Passion 7 Stages of Course Creation clearly outline the path of how a client gets the outcome they want – a suite of products that leverage their expertise, allowing them to work one-to-many and make a real difference.

Ask yourself:
- Where is your Ideal Client now (before you start working with them)?
- What has to happen to get my Ideal Client from where they are now to where they want to be?
- What do they need to learn?
- What do they need to understand?
- What actions do they need to take?

One of my favourite ways to approach developing this, is to use post-it notes and write one idea on each one. Then stick them up on the wall and arrange them into "chunks" or stages.

Remember, to focus on giving this your best thinking now. It can and probably will evolve. To help to fine tune your Steps & Stages, ask yourself the following questions:
- Can these steps and stages be chunked or arranged in another way?
- Is this the simplest and clearest process?
- Do any of these steps or stages actually apply across the whole process? If they do, they might actually be "principles" rather than steps or stages.

Obstacles

Quite simply, the Obstacles element is about defining and illustrating the biggest challenges or barriers your clients face in achieving their outcome. In clearly articulating their biggest obstacles to success, we can then demonstrate how to overcome them.

Let's look at the barriers to Wholehearted Living and the Principles you can embrace to overcome them.

beware the eight barriers!	wholehearted living principles
unhealthy relationships	thriving relationships
fear	growth mindset
lack of leverage	get leverage
lack of action	action plan & accountability
limiting beliefs	empowering beliefs
stuck in the story	live in gratitude in the moment
the blame game	take responsibility & live at cause
lack of clarity	get clear

STAGE 4: BLUEPRINT

Barriers	Principles
Lack of Clarity A lack of clarity about who you really are and what you stand for can be debilitating.	**Get Clear** "I have a clear sense of self and purpose." Being able to clearly articulate who you are, what you stand for and your purpose will give you an amazing sense of confidence and certainty.
The Blame Game Blaming others, playing the victim and not taking responsibility for your own life is disempowering.	**Take Responsibility and Live at Cause** "I take responsibility for all aspects of my life and acknowledge that the quality of my life is up to me." Taking responsibility for the choices in your life and your situation is extremely empowering.
Being Stuck in the Story Replaying or reliving the stories and scenarios from your past can imprison you and make you miserable.	**Live in Gratitude in the Moment** "I am living with a spirit of gratitude, grounded and present." Gratitude, forgiveness and acceptance will set you free. It might sound "airy fairy", but when put into practice, will give you an amazing sense of power.
Limiting Beliefs Limiting beliefs are those beliefs and expectations (from ourselves and others) that don't serve us. They are the "shoulds" and "expectations" that prevent us from living our lives our way.	**Empowering Beliefs** "My empowering beliefs and self-talk are congruent with my ultimate vision for myself and my purpose." Overcoming your limiting beliefs about yourself and handling "shoulds" and "expectations" (from self and others), replacing them with a set of empowering beliefs.

Lack of Action Knowing what to do and doing what you know are two different things. Without a plan and structure in place to hold you accountable, fear and procrastination take over.	**Clear Action Plan and Accountability** "I have a clear specific action plan with deadlines and I am being held accountable to it." Having a clear action plan and being held accountable to it will ensure that your career transition is not just a dream, it's a reality.
Lack of Leverage Sometimes the suffering we're experiencing in our dry barren paddock isn't strong enough to push us into making the necessary changes. The grass on the other side doesn't seem green enough for us to jump the fence.	**Get Leverage** "I have the motivation to do whatever it takes." Overcoming the "better the devil you know" syndrome! This involves a psychological shift.
Fear Being afraid of what others will think, the risks, money, fear of failure, fear of success, etc.	**Growth Mindset** "I am embracing the fear, learning the lessons and making conscious choices." Embracing fear and adopting a growth mindset won't stop fear arising, but it will ensure that it doesn't hold you back.
Unhealthy Relationships These can hold you back and feeling unfulfilled can contribute to unhealthy relationships. It's a potential relationship crisis cycle.	**Thriving Relationships** "I am nurturing thriving relationships that nurture me." Creating thriving relationships will get things on track!

Ask yourself: What gets in the way of my clients getting the results that they want? What do they need to do to overcome these obstacles?

Elements

Elements represent all the pieces of the puzzle or the building blocks that your client needs. There are times when things don't necessarily happen in a clear step-by-step process. When there are a number of elements that are all important and they all seemingly need attention simultaneously.

For example, in a business, all the areas of a business need to be addressed at the same time. You don't do Marketing in Stage 1, Finance in Stage 2, and so on. You need to be spinning all those plates at the same time. This is where it is more appropriate to represent chunks of information as elements or spheres.

In your program, sometimes these elements will become the top level framework and sometimes they will become a framework within one of the Stages or modules.

The Share Your Passion Marketing elements is an example of this.

Ask yourself: What are all the pieces of the puzzle that my client needs to achieve success?

Success Criteria

An important element in developing your intellectual property is defining your Success Criteria. The purpose of Success Criteria is to provide your clients with a checklist to either set themselves up for success or to evaluate their progress or choice.

An example of Success Criteria is the Passion Sweet Spot. When someone is considering a business idea or career, it gives them a methodology or framework to evaluate it.

STAGE 4: BLUEPRINT

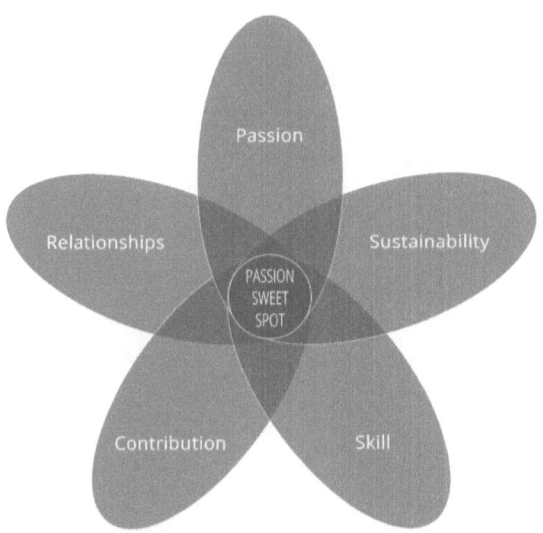

Ask yourself: What criteria will set your clients up for success? And, what criteria can your clients use to evaluate their success?

Modules

The final element of developing the basics of your intellectual property or Blueprint is listing your Modules. These are the learning Modules that your clients will undertake. There are two main ways that these are usually broken down. Either following the Steps & Stages you have developed *or* following your elements model.

Action
- ✓ Create Your **Value Model**
- ✓ Create Your **Stages & Steps**

- ✓ Define Your Client's Biggest **Obstacles**
- ✓ Outline the **Elements**
- ✓ Define **Success Criteria**
- ✓ List Your **Modules**
- ✓ Design Infographics for each element of your Blueprint

Want the full 7 Stages of Course Creation action checklist all in one document? You can download it at shareyourpassion.com.au/7-stages-checklist

STAGE 5: FRAME IT

Whatever good things we build end up building us.

Jim Rohn

Stage 5: Frame It

Woo hoo! You've made it to Stage 5, I knew you could do this. Now although I get really excited about Stage 4 because that is where you get to really express who you are through your own unique intellectual property, Stage 5 is where you can start to see it all taking shape. This is where you frame the modules for your course.

By outlining and thinking about this first, you'll avoid going round in circles getting bamboozled by all your own knowledge when you start building!

Once you get this stage done, you can outsource the building stage to an instructional designer or do it yourself.

Before you get started, remember to get in the zone for brainstorming.

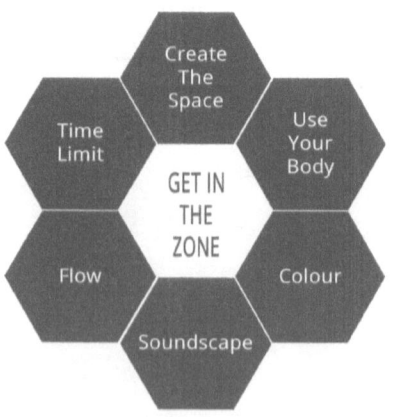

Frame Your Modules

Framing your modules includes defining your learning objectives and outcomes, as well as determining the bullet points, topics, checklists, top tips, learning exercises, statistics, research, case studies, examples and stories that are relevant for each module.

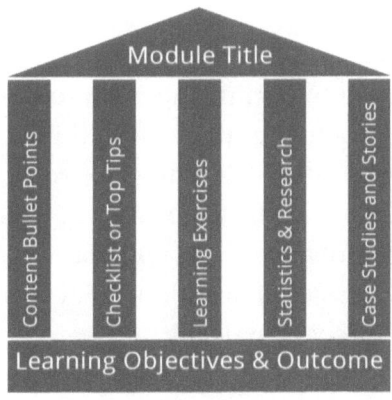

Get the Foundations Right

Getting clear on the learning objectives and outcome is critical to laying the foundations for your course frame. So, for the course as a whole and then for each of your modules, define what you want your clients to learn and what the outcome is.

You'll also want to be able to illustrate how each module fits into the bigger picture. Your course should be based on either the steps & stages or elements you created in Stage 4 – Blueprint, so it should be really obvious how it all fits together.

When you have an infographic that clearly shows how a chunk of information fits into the bigger picture, your clients know how to sort it and file it in their minds.

The Pillars

Next, you need to outline the main topics you want to cover in each module. Also, think about any checklists or top tips, learning exercises, statistics & research, case studies, stories and examples you will include. Not all of these will apply for all topics, but it helps to ask the questions to get you thinking through the process logically.

I personally find that it helps to use a spreadsheet to lay this out.

The table below is an example of how you might do this.

STAGE 5: FRAME IT

Topic	Bullet Points	Checklist or Top Tips	Learning Exercises	Statistics & Research	Case Studies, Stories or Examples

Action

For each of your modules, outline:
- ✓ Module Title
- ✓ Learning Objectives & Outcome
- ✓ How Does This Module Fit Into The Bigger Picture? (Infographic is great here)
- ✓ Content Bullet Points
- ✓ Checklist Or Top Tips (e.g.: Biggest Mistakes, Keys to Success, etc.)
- ✓ Learning Exercises
- ✓ Statistics & Research
- ✓ Case Studies & Stories

Want the full 7 Stages of Course Creation action checklist all in one document? You can download it at shareyourpassion.com.au/7-stages-checklist

STAGE 6:
BUILD IT

If you build it they will come... but only if you've laid the right foundations.

Renée Hasseldine

Stage 6: Build It

If you build it they will come... but only if you've laid the right foundations. I don't want to walk into a building with rocky foundations. It might come crumbling down on me. In the same way, I don't want to walk into a business that hasn't laid the foundations securely, whether I'm there as an owner, consultant, or customer. If you've been playing along at home, and working through each of the first five stages, then you've been laying the foundations upon which to build a really solid program. Well done you!

How long does building the modules take? How long is a piece of string?

But as a rough estimate, you can work on the following guide per discrete topic:
- worksheet (2-3 hours)
- slides (1-2 hours)
- video (1 hour – if applicable)

So that's 3-6 hours per topic. This is just an average and it will depend on many factors. Some topics flow easier than others and some contain more content than others. Some will be quick and easy and some take more of a concerted effort.

Stage 6 is by far the most time-consuming of the stages. As I mentioned, most people come to me just

STAGE 6: BUILD IT

wanting to jump straight into this stage. Jumping in here is highly dangerous, and often the reason people take years to develop their course or never actually get it finished. But if you've been a diligent student and completed Stages 1-5, you've set yourself up to complete this in the most efficient way.

Stick to the plan. Stick to your framework and don't go off on tangents. It's okay to go back and update your framework if you need to, but beware getting dragged into black holes. Stay focused and get in the zone! Set yourself clear time limits and targets for each resource.

There are four steps to this stage as shown in the diagram below.

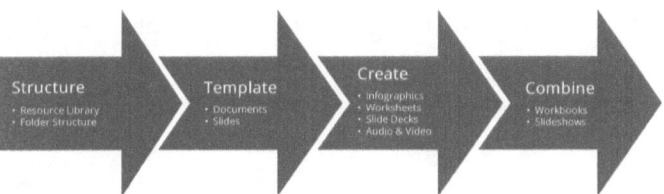

Structure

There are a couple of things that need to happen to get the structure in place for creating your content.

A great way to keep track of all the resources you create is in a Resource Library Spreadsheet. You might end up with a couple hundred resources (worksheets, slideshows, etc.) and a spreadsheet can help to ensure you don't get lost in it all.

I like to start by listing all the resources I'm going to create – one for each topic. I also like to use codes for my resources as I find that is a quick way to refer to them for both myself and when speaking with others. Especially if you're going to get help from team members such as instructional designers, designers, virtual assistants, etc.

I've found that having well designed templates for my worksheets and slideshows means I can avoid paying designers to format resources. I do still delegate fiddly bits especially when tedious work is not a good use of my time. For example, I love having big images on my slides with only a few words. Finding the right images is one of those tasks that you can lose hours down a rabbit hole on. So that's something I love to delegate.

I've used the spreadsheet below for clients and now I'm using it to build my own courses. If you are collaborating with your team, consider setting this up as a Google Sheet so you all have access to the most up-to-date version in real-time.

STAGE 6: BUILD IT

Here's a snapshot of a working spreadsheet:

Code	Name	Drafts		Worksheet Delegation			Slides Delegation		Final Resources Created			
		Worksheet	Slides	Who to?	Date		Who to?	Date	MS Word	PDF	Slides	Video
S1-01	Introduction to Stage 1	Yes		NA	NA				Yes	Yes		
S1-02	Why? Who? What?	Yes		NA	NA				Yes	Yes		
S1-03	Why? Passion & Purpose	Yes		NA	NA				Yes	Yes		
S1-04	Why? Values	Yes		NA	NA				Yes	Yes		
S1-05	Why? Vision	yes		NA	NA				Yes	Yes		
S1-06	Why? Compelling Story	Yes		NA	NA				Yes	Yes		
S1-0Seven	Who?	Yes		NA	NA				Yes	Yes		
S1-08	What?	Yes		NA	NA				Yes	Yes		

I have a separate tab that looks like this for each module. Identify all the topics you will cover for each module. I recommend each topic is created as a separate resource. This avoids having multiple copies of the same information. You can then pull together multiple PDFs to create workbooks for various courses/events as required.

Having a well-organised Folder Structure makes all the difference when you are creating resources en masse. I use something like this:

- Artwork
  - Module 1
  - Module 2
  - Module 3
  - Module 4
  - Etc..
  - Logo

- Worksheets
  - Module 1
    PDFs of the worksheets here.
    - Design
      Word Versions of the worksheets stored here.
  - Module 2
    PDFs of the worksheets here.
    - Design
      Word Versions of the worksheets stored here.

- Etc.
- Slides
  - Module 1
    Separate slideshow files for each topic here.
  - Module 2
    Separate slideshow files for each topic here.
  - Etc.
- Products
  - Workshop 1
    Combined PDF "Workbook" & slideshow here.
  - Workshop 2
    Combined PDF "Workbook" & slideshow here.
  - Etc.

Template

As I've already mentioned, having well-designed templates for your worksheets and slideshows will save you time and money. I had a client who was paying thousands of dollars to a graphic designer to create his worksheets for every event he ran. He would type up what he wanted in a word doc, then he would send it to her and she would make it look great in InDesign. Then the worksheets would come back and need to be proofread again. For one particular event, it took about three rounds of proofing for the designer to get it right.

In my honest opinion this was a great example of over-engineering and not a great use of time and money. It was also extremely frustrating for my client whose money was going down the drain and for me to see him doing things the hard way.

Addressing this was critical to my client's profit and sanity, and simply involved us implementing a new, efficient process. His worksheet creation now happens the easy way, using the process I've outlined here. By creating word templates that looked equivalent to the InDesign documents, my client can enter content directly into the template and it automatically looks like it should. It's more efficient and this simple innovation has already saved him thousands of dollars.

Create

When you're writing the content for your slides and worksheets, it can help to use this framework as a guide:
- **Why** is this important?
- **Who** is this for?
- **When** does it apply?
- **Where** does it fit in?
- **What** to do?
- **How** to do it?

As you start creating the worksheets and developing your topics, you will need to create more diagrams or infographics. When you've got a whole heap of content, think about how you can organize and chunk it into a process (steps and stages) or elements and represent it graphically. It helps to have this visual representation for your clients to understand how things fit together and also to make it memorable.

Start working through your resource library and create the worksheets. Keep each topic as a separate word file and export it to PDF.

My hot tip here is to start by creating your checklist first. If you create a checklist for your whole program, you have your "free product" or opt-in ready to go *and* it makes creating your worksheets and detailed content much easier.

I've written the whole first draft for this book in three consecutive days. And the reason it was possible to do this, besides having an amazing support team, is because my 7 Stages Checklist formed the basis of what I needed to cover.

In the same way, that checklist is what I'm using to create the content for my VIP group program.

When you're working on your slide decks, keep each topic as a separate slideshow file, just as you created separate worksheets for each topic. You can then just pull together the topics you need for each event. This means that if you want to update anything, you update the main topic file, so that is always the most up-to-date.

If you are going to be creating an online course, then the next step is to record and edit the audio and/or video. However, if you are new to running this content, as I mentioned when discussing the product funnel in Stage 3, I recommend you start off by running a live group program first. Get the feedback you need from running it at least once or twice and once it is tweaked, then you can record it for an online course. Or perhaps you can even use the recordings from your group program.

Combine

So once you've created your worksheets and slides for each topic, you now have a full resource library from which to pull together each of your products.

For example, I can create a workbook for Stage 1 by pulling together all the PDFs in that section. Alternatively, I might only choose to use one or two of those worksheets for a lower-end version of my content.

I combine my PDFs in Adobe Acrobat. If I have to edit anything, I don't edit the final workbook. I go back to the original worksheet in word format, edit it and export it to PDF again. I then reinsert the updated PDF into the workbook.

That way, I can be confident that when I'm pulling together workbooks in the future, the single topic worksheet is always the most up-to-date.

The same theory applies for your slideshows. Pull together the topics you need for your webinars, group calls, or live events. And if you need to update any slides, update the original topic slides and reinsert them into the combined file. Make it easy on yourself by becoming systematic!

Action
- ✓ Create a Resource Library Spreadsheet
- ✓ Create your Folder Structure
- ✓ Create a Word (or equivalent) Template for your Worksheets. You may like a different template for each module. i.e. a Template with the Module Heading on it.
- ✓ Create a Slideshow Template (Powerpoint, Keynote, Prezi) for your presentations.
- ✓ Design and Create Infographics
- ✓ Create the Worksheets. Remember to keep each topic as a separate word file and export it to PDF.
- ✓ Create the Slide Decks. Remember to keep each topic as a separate slideshow file. You can then just pull together the topics you need for each event.

- ✓ Record the Audio/Video
- ✓ Edit the Audio/Video
- ✓ Pull together Worksheet PDFs for Product Workbooks
- ✓ Pull together Topic slideshows

Want the full 7 Stages of Course Creation action checklist all in one document? You can download it at shareyourpassion.com.au/7-stages-checklist

STAGE 7: DELIVER

The more they feel, the more they will learn. You are teaching people not robots.

Renée Hasseldine

Stage 7: Deliver

Know your Audience

We've already talked about the importance of being really clear about your Ideal Client. When you come to the delivery stage, you need to revisit this. Get to know your audience intimately. If you don't know what they're thinking, what they want or need, then ask them. Talk to them. Interview them. Survey them.

When you're presenting to an audience, it's critical that you understand where they are at. My gorgeous husband teaches high school students and I admire and respect him for this. I can't imagine dealing with a room full of hormone fuelled teenagers who would rather be somewhere else and who often can't see the point of what they are learning. The idea of trying to command their attention scares me.

And I'm no better with primary school students! My daughter started primary school this year. I volunteer as "class helper" on Tuesday mornings for less than two hours. Let's just say that this has been a humbling experience. I have the utmost respect and admiration for my daughter's teacher, Mrs Lisa Pascal. She is so softly spoken and calm, but when she speaks, the children respect and respond. Meanwhile, on the table I'm assisting with, with a maximum of six Prep kids (5 or 6 years old),

I'm struggling with the juggling act of behaviour management and helping the kids to get their work done. In less than two hours, I'm exhausted.

On the other hand, give me a room full of super smart, experienced conscious entrepreneurs and I'll have the time of my life! I'll thrive and feel pumped, knowing I'm making a difference. When you know your audience, you can speak their language, pitch the learning at the right level and facilitate awesome results.

Build in Testing & Learning Over Time

Testing (including self-testing) improves learning & retention because of the active attention and emotional impact testing involves. Communication among neurons is strengthened and that helps embed newly learned information into memory. Learning becomes durable.

To make a real difference with your clients, find ways to build testing into your courses where possible and appropriate.

In a Washington University study, two groups of students were given some material to learn. Both studied it for a set period of time. Then one group was given more time to study and a second group did a test on the material. Both groups were then given a recall test – after five minutes, after two days and after one week.

The results are shown in the table below:

	STUDY STUDY	STUDY TEST
After 5 min:	81%	Seven5%
After 2 days:	54%	68%
After 1 week:	42%	56%

Ref: 2006 – Roediger et al. Washington University

Prof John Dunlovsky, of Kent State University and his colleagues reviewed 1,000 scientific studies looking at ten of the most popular revision strategies. Eight out of ten of those techniques didn't work and some even hindered learning!

The table below illustrates a summary of their findings.

Technique	Description	Effectiveness
Elaborative interrogation	being able to explain a point or fact	MODERATE
Self-explanation	how a problem was solved	MODERATE
Summarising	writing summaries of texts	LOW
Highlighting/ underlining		LOW

Keyword mnemonics	choosing a word to associate with information	LOW
Imagery	forming mental pictures while reading or listening	LOW
Re-reading		LOW
Practice testing	self-testing to check knowledge, especially using flash cards	HIGH
Distributed practice	spreading out study over time	HIGH
Interleaved practice	switching between different kinds of problems	MODERATE

The results are in. Practice testing and distributed practice are the most effective study techniques. So, if you want your students to learn for long-term results, then find ways to build testing into your courses and spread the learnings out over time.

So, what are you going to do to integrate testing and distributed practice into your courses?

A Note about Learning Styles

The research shows that different learning styles, such as kinaesthetic, visual and auditory, are not necessarily appropriate or applicable for different people but appropriate for different concepts. So if you're teaching children how to count, holding objects will improve their learning. Not because a person is kinesthetic but because this is an effective way to learn to count.

So when selecting how you will teach each topic, consider which strategies will be most effective for that lesson or concept. Refer back to the learning objectives and outcome. Brainstorm the possibilities. Test and tweak.

Keep them Awake

For your students to get the best value from your teaching and create real change in their lives and businesses, you, at the very least, have to keep them awake.

Actually you're going to have to set a higher standard than this! Not only do you have to keep them awake, you have to keep them engaged in the learning process.

The more they feel, the more they will learn.

You are teaching people not robots.

I mentioned in the first part of this book that I slept through most university lectures. Please, I beg of you. Don't be like my boring micro-economics lecturer.

I promise it's not me. I have listened to amazing facilitators and inspiring thought leaders for hours and days on end and not fallen asleep once. And I was a pretty damn good student in primary and secondary school. I don't remember falling asleep there either. Okay, I shouldn't say I was a "good" student but I can honestly say I was awake. Maybe a bit of a trouble-maker. But that's a story for another time. The point I'm making is, for the teachers out there, if I fall asleep, it's not me, it's you.

I barely remember anything I "learned" at university. On the other hand, the learnings from my experience as a participant and Senior Leader with Tony Robbins have been integrated and implemented into who I am today.

So how can you keep your students awake? Make them feel something!

You must engage them, get them to apply and implement the knowledge, discuss and debate ideas, move and use their bodies. Fire up your students and make them feel something.

Being an inspiring teacher doesn't mean having all the answers. Don't let your ego and the sound of your own voice get in the way of awesome results.

Let the learning objectives and outcomes guide the lesson plan.

Here are some ideas:
- ✓ Ice-breakers.
- ✓ Games. They can be as simple or complex, as fun or as thought provoking as you like.

Tie the games into the learning by debriefing them at the end.
- ✓ Dancing. Have people take turns to lead.
- ✓ Massage trains.
- ✓ Conga lines.
- ✓ Pair work. Get them standing up for this and walking away from their seat.
- ✓ Group work. Standing will increase energy levels.
- ✓ Implementation. Get them to apply the information to their own situation immediately.
- ✓ Hot–seats. Get people to ask their questions live and respond. Working through a real life example or challenge.
- ✓ Mastermind – sharing progress or responses with the group and getting constructive feedback.
- ✓ Perspective spectrum – present a scenario or case study. Pose a question, for or against. Where do you stand? Physically stand on the line. Ask people why they are where they are. Gives a picture of the spectrum of perspectives.
- ✓ Group work – Establish small work groups for activities, giving individuals specific roles in the group. You could break this up in a variety of ways, for example:
    i. Company Job Titles (CEO, CFO, Marketing Director, Receptionist, Sales Manager, etc.)

ii. Debono's Six Thinking Hats (white hat=facts, green hat=creativity, yellow hat=benefits, black hat=cautions, red hat=feelings, and blue hat=process)
- ✓ Brainstorming. Ask quality questions and write responses on a flip chart or white board before you share your own perspective.

Go out there and be the inspiring teacher who sees their students as human beings and ignites their passion and desire for learning and growth.

Action

Maximise Results
- ✓ Know your Audience
- ✓ Build in Implementation
- ✓ Build in Testing where possible and appropriate

Discovery Sessions
- ✓ Develop a framework for running your discovery sessions

VIP Group Programs
- ✓ Determine which conferencing or webinar platform you will use to run your VIP Group Program (e.g. Zoom)
- ✓ Setup your conferencing platform and test it
- ✓ Determine how you will distribute workbooks and recorded material. i.e. via email or through a membership site

- ✓ Schedule the material distribution, i.e. create the emails to distribute workbooks if using this method, or set them up to "drip feed" through your membership site
- ✓ Create a Welcome email for your clients
- ✓ Create an email detailing the Live Call information
- ✓ Create the Sales Funnel
- ✓ Prepare Your Slides for each Call (if applicable)
- ✓ Launch/Promote the Program

Online Courses
- ✓ Determine which Online Platform you will use to deliver your course. There's no one-size-fits-all solution. There are so many options available. You can spend many tens of hours (or more) researching and testing various platforms.
- ✓ Setup the Learning Platform
- ✓ Load the Material (e.g.: each topic as a separate lesson with PDF and video)
- ✓ Create the Sales Funnel
- ✓ Launch/Promote the Course

Live Events
- ✓ Set the Dates and Times
- ✓ Book the Venue. Another possible rabbit hole! I would personally get on a Facebook group, list my requirements and ask for rec-

ommended venues. That should hopefully give you a short list.
- ✓ Create the Sales Funnel.
- ✓ Launch/Promote the Event.
- ✓ Make sure you have a Live Event Logistics Checklist.
- ✓ Create Your Workbook files combining individual PDFs into a combined PDF workbook.
- ✓ Get Workbooks printed.
- ✓ Create Your Slideshows combining individual topics into full workshop files.

Want the full 7 Stages of Course Creation action checklist all in one document? You can download it at shareyourpassion.com.au/7-stages-checklist

CONCLUSION

We make a living by what we get, but we make a life by what we give.

Winston Churchill

Congratulations! You've made it through the 7 Stages of Course Creation, and I hope you've been motivated to work through each step to completion. You may not have the final product in your hand yet, but you have to make a start. Somewhere. Then you can return and re-work, refine and evolve what you've got. Remember you are unique, brilliant and capable so get out of your own way and let your star light up the sky.

Of course, there are other streams involved in running your business. There are the marketing & sales, leadership & team, and finance & admin streams to cover. But those topics are for another day (and maybe another book)!

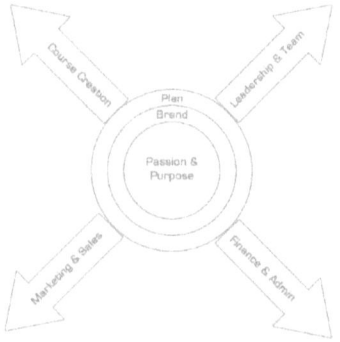

CONCLUSION

Our deepest fear is not that we are inadequate

Our deepest fear is that we are powerful beyond measure

It is our light, not our darkness, that frightens us.

We ask ourselves, who am I to be brilliant, gorgeous, talented, and famous?

Actually, who are you not to be?

You are a child of God.

Your playing small doesn't serve the world.

There's nothing enlightened about shrinking so that other people won't feel insecure around you.

We were born to manifest the glory of God that is within us.

It is not just in some of us, it's in everyone.

And as we let our own light shine we unconsciously give other people permission to do the same.

As we are liberated from our own fears, our presence automatically liberates others.

Marianne Williamson

ACKNOWLEDGEMENTS

Thank you firstly to my wonderful husband for wholeheartedly supporting me when I suggested I would write this book. You're always by my side Ant and I wouldn't have it any other way. You make a difference in people's lives every day and I have so much love and respect for the contribution you make. The world is a better place because you're in it.

To our wonderful daughters Callista and Cinta – thank you for giving me even more reason to get serious and nail the purpose of my work. If I'm going to spend time away from you, I'd better be doing something worthwhile! I love you to the stars and back times infinity.

To the clients who have inspired me by who they are and what they stand for, I'll always be grateful. In particular, I want to thank Jan Spaticchia for those grassy knoll days and Dr Jesse Green for the opportunities to have fun getting shit done.

Thanks to my Dad who gave me my first personal development books. It takes a cool Dad to present his teenage daughter with "How To Win Friends And Influence People", "The 7 Habits of Highly Effective People", "Rich Dad, Poor Dad" and more.

Thanks to my Mum who is always there to pick up the pieces when I bite off more than I can chew and am ready to fall in a heap. You're always there to help look after the kids, or prepare a meal and I couldn't do it all without you.

To my friend Nigel "Will" Polak... In the midst of my depression, you were the housemate who was there for me. Who got me through the darkest days... and then dragged me along to my first Tony Robbins event. The rest is history and some might say it is all your fault!

To my friend and colleague Carolyn Farrow who always sees the best in me and knows me like no other. Thanks for "getting" me and not being scared off after all these years. Thanks for your absolute honesty and truth. It is a rare and precious gift that I cherish deeply. Thanks for dropping everything and staying up late to proofread my book. May we grow old, but hopefully not incontinent together!

Thanks to Alitta Berson, "Rebecca" and Fiona Livingwell for sharing your stories with me and to all my lovely friends who supported me through this journey through social media.

To Dave Thompson for creating the Inspirational Book Writers' Retreat. What a treat. You truly are creating something fantastic with the Spiritcast Network and I know it will continue to grow from

ACKNOWLEDGEMENTS

strength to strength. To any budding authors out there, I highly recommend investing seven days of your life to finally get your book written and get your message out there.

To Dave Thompson, Matt Gardner and Benjamin Reeves for the amazing support during the retreat. Your coaching, cheerleading, proofreading, honest feedback, coffee runs, cooking, cleaning, bath running and company allowed me to drop into writing and to reconnect with my true self.

To my fellow book writers Dane Tomas, Suzy Jukes, Tara Davidson and Lionel Fowler. What a week! I don't think we knew what we were getting ourselves into, but I'm glad we did! Oh and special thanks to Dane for clearing my emotional blockages so I could hit the ground running on the first day of writing and to Tara for getting me out of my "funk" on Friday night.

ABOUT THE AUTHOR

Renée is the awesome mum of two sensational little girls. Her third baby is *Share Your Passion*. Simply put, she is unequivocally passionate about enabling you to share your own mission in the most effective and productive way.

Renée is a highly evolved, super smart original. While she's definitely one of a kind, to help you out, think Erin Brokovich (fights for justice), mixed with Thich Nhat Hanh (Zen Master), and throw in just a little Pink (superbly wicked) for good measure.

When it comes to course creation, Renée is a superstar. Her knack for extracting powerful ideas and transforming them into succinct, inspired content is sheer brilliance. This is the core of *Share Your Passion*, and it is a critical skill for any visionary who is ready to take their message to the world.

Renée is a committed advocate for the environment, the underdog and bullet proof coffee. Her enthusiasm for low budget vampire dramas is a little disturbing.

When you meet Renée, expect her take on things to be a little different and her expression to be unique. Both are authentic and spot on. Oh, and order your own piece of cake.

FIND ME ONLINE

http://shareyourpassion.com.au

http://www.facebook.com/ipassetqueen

https://twitter.com/ipassetqueen

ABOUT SHARE YOUR PASSION

Our Purpose:

Empowering people to love what they do and do what they love.

Our Values:

Passion:
Our core philosophy is "Having Fun Getting Shit Done." It means loving what WE do and doing what we love. We F.L.O.W. (Freaking Love Our Work). Our golden rule is that we will only pursue projects with meaning and purpose, and that we can authentically complete it with integrity.

Sustainability:
For self, others and the planet. This means all pursuits must serve the individual on a physical, mental, spiritual, emotional and financial level. We will only undertake opportunities in a way that nurtures and serves others. We desire to contribute to the greater good, making our personal space, business community, and ultimately the planet a more authentic, joyful place.

Results:

Our objective is to achieve *your* outcomes and solve *your* problems, efficiently and effectively. We produce thoughtful work of a high standard, aiming to exceed expectations. This means completing projects on time, on budget, and with lots of fun. Every time.

Vision:

Igniting the passion in thought leaders to package their brilliance into products people love, through group programs, speaking engagements, retreats and online courses.

RESOURCES

I have a range of free resources, including checklists and self-assessments available on my website.

You'll find them at shareyourpassion.com.au/services/resources

WORK WITH ME

Are you ready to own your zone of genius and be the go-to expert in your field?

To find out how we can work together, go to shareyourpassion.com.au/services or send me an email to renee@shareyourpassion.com.au

NOTES

NOTES

NOTES

NOTES

NOTES

NOTES

NOTES

NOTES

NOTES

NOTES

www.ingramcontent.com/pod-product-compliance
Lightning Source LLC
Chambersburg PA
CBHW031117080526
44587CB00011B/1006